Baby Logbook

THIS BOOK BELONGS TO

Baby's Mood

DATE

FOOD

AM

Time	Food	Amount

PM

Time	Food	Amount

SLEEP

AM

Start	End	Duration

PM

Start	End	Duration

DIAPER

Pee Poop Time

Pee Poop Time

Activity Notes

Baby's Mood 😁 ☹ 😌 😐 😠

DATE

FOOD

AM

Time	Food	Amount

PM

Time	Food	Amount

SLEEP

AM

Start	End	Duration

PM

Start	End	Duration

DIAPER

Pee Poop   Time

○ ○ __________
○ ○ __________
○ ○ __________

Pee Poop   Time

○ ○ __________
○ ○ __________
○ ○ __________

Activity Notes

Baby's Mood

DATE

AM   FOOD   PM

Time	Food	Amount		Time	Food	Amount

AM   SLEEP   PM

Start	End	Duration		Start	End	Duration

DIAPER

Pee Poop Time   Pee Poop Time

O O ————   O O ————

O O ————   O O ————

O O ————   O O ————

Activity Notes

Baby's Mood

FOOD

AM

Time	Food	Amount

PM

Time	Food	Amount

SLEEP

AM

Start	End	Duration

PM

Start	End	Duration

DIAPER

Pee	Poop	Time
○	○	
○	○	
○	○	

Pee	Poop	Time
○	○	
○	○	
○	○	

Activity Notes

Baby's Mood 😁 ☹️ 😌 😐 😠

<table>
<tr><td colspan="3"></td><td>DATE</td></tr>
</table>

FOOD

	AM			**PM**	
Time	Food	Amount	Time	Food	Amount

SLEEP

	AM			**PM**	
Start	End	Duration	Start	End	Duration

DIAPER

Pee	Poop	Time		Pee	Poop	Time
○	○			○	○	
○	○			○	○	
○	○			○	○	

Activity Notes

Baby's Mood

DATE

FOOD

AM

Time	Food	Amount

PM

Time	Food	Amount

SLEEP

AM

Start	End	Duration

PM

Start	End	Duration

DIAPER

Pee	Poop	Time
O	O	
O	O	
O	O	

Pee	Poop	Time
O	O	
O	O	
O	O	

Activity Notes

Baby's Mood

DATE

FOOD

AM

Time	Food	Amount

PM

Time	Food	Amount

SLEEP

AM

Start	End	Duration

PM

Start	End	Duration

DIAPER

Pee	Poop	Time
○	○	
○	○	
○	○	

Pee	Poop	Time
○	○	
○	○	
○	○	

Activity Notes

Baby's Mood

😁 ☹ 😌 😐 😠

DATE

FOOD

AM

Time	Food	Amount

PM

Time	Food	Amount

SLEEP

AM

Start	End	Duration

PM

Start	End	Duration

DIAPER

Pee	Poop	Time
○	○	
○	○	
○	○	

Pee	Poop	Time
○	○	
○	○	
○	○	

Activity Notes

Baby's Mood 😁 ☹ 😌 😐 😠

FOOD

AM

Time	Food	Amount

PM

Time	Food	Amount

SLEEP

AM

Start	End	Duration

PM

Start	End	Duration

DIAPER

Pee Poop Time

Pee Poop Time

Activity Notes

Baby's Mood 😁 ☹ 😌 😐 😠

FOOD

AM

Time	Food	Amount

PM

Time	Food	Amount

SLEEP

AM

Start	End	Duration

PM

Start	End	Duration

DIAPER

Pee	Poop	Time
O	O	
O	O	
O	O	

Pee	Poop	Time
O	O	
O	O	
O	O	

Activity Notes

Baby's Mood

DATE

FOOD

AM

Time	Food	Amount

PM

Time	Food	Amount

SLEEP

AM

Start	End	Duration

PM

Start	End	Duration

DIAPER

Pee	Poop	Time		Pee	Poop	Time
○	○			○	○	
○	○			○	○	
○	○			○	○	

Activity Notes

Baby's Mood

DATE

FOOD

	AM				PM	
Time	Food	Amount		Time	Food	Amount

SLEEP

	AM				PM	
Start	End	Duration		Start	End	Duration

DIAPER

Pee Poop Time

Pee Poop Time

Activity Notes

Baby's Mood

DATE

FOOD

AM

Time	Food	Amount

PM

Time	Food	Amount

SLEEP

AM

Start	End	Duration

PM

Start	End	Duration

DIAPER

Pee Poop Time

Pee Poop Time

Activity Notes

Baby's Mood 😁 ☹ 😌 😐 😠

FOOD

AM

Time	Food	Amount

PM

Time	Food	Amount

SLEEP

AM

Start	End	Duration

PM

Start	End	Duration

DIAPER

Pee	Poop	Time
○	○	
○	○	
○	○	

Pee	Poop	Time
○	○	
○	○	
○	○	

Activity Notes

Baby's Mood

DATE

FOOD

AM

Time	Food	Amount

PM

Time	Food	Amount

SLEEP

AM

Start	End	Duration

PM

Start	End	Duration

DIAPER

Pee	Poop	Time
◯	◯	
◯	◯	
◯	◯	

Pee	Poop	Time
◯	◯	
◯	◯	
◯	◯	

Activity Notes

Baby's Mood

😁 ☹ 😌 😐 😠

DATE

FOOD

AM

Time	Food	Amount

PM

Time	Food	Amount

SLEEP

AM

Start	End	Duration

PM

Start	End	Duration

DIAPER

Pee	Poop	Time
○	○	
○	○	
○	○	

Pee	Poop	Time
○	○	
○	○	
○	○	

Activity Notes

Baby's Mood

FOOD

AM
Time	Food	Amount

PM
Time	Food	Amount

SLEEP

AM
Start	End	Duration

PM
Start	End	Duration

DIAPER

Pee Poop Time

Pee Poop Time

Activity Notes

Baby's Mood

😁 ☹ 😌 😐 😠

FOOD

AM

Time	Food	Amount

PM

Time	Food	Amount

SLEEP

AM

Start	End	Duration

PM

Start	End	Duration

DIAPER

Pee	Poop	Time		Pee	Poop	Time
○	○			○	○	
○	○			○	○	
○	○			○	○	

Activity Notes

Baby's Mood

FOOD

AM

Time	Food	Amount

PM

Time	Food	Amount

SLEEP

AM

Start	End	Duration

PM

Start	End	Duration

DIAPER

Pee Poop   Time

Pee Poop   Time

Activity Notes

Baby's Mood

😁 ☹️ 😌 😐 😠

FOOD

AM

Time	Food	Amount
______	______	______
______	______	______
______	______	______
______	______	______
______	______	______
______	______	______

PM

Time	Food	Amount
______	______	______
______	______	______
______	______	______
______	______	______
______	______	______
______	______	______

SLEEP

AM

Start	End	Duration
______	______	______
______	______	______
______	______	______
______	______	______
______	______	______

PM

Start	End	Duration
______	______	______
______	______	______
______	______	______
______	______	______
______	______	______

DIAPER

Pee	Poop	Time
◯	◯	______
◯	◯	______
◯	◯	______

Pee	Poop	Time
◯	◯	______
◯	◯	______
◯	◯	______

Activity Notes

Baby's Mood

FOOD

AM

Time	Food	Amount

PM

Time	Food	Amount

SLEEP

AM

Start	End	Duration

PM

Start	End	Duration

DIAPER

Pee Poop Time

Pee Poop Time

Activity Notes

Baby's Mood

DATE

FOOD

AM

Time	Food	Amount

PM

Time	Food	Amount

SLEEP

AM

Start	End	Duration

PM

Start	End	Duration

DIAPER

Pee	Poop	Time
○	○	
○	○	
○	○	

Pee	Poop	Time
○	○	
○	○	
○	○	

Activity Notes

Baby's Mood

DATE

FOOD

AM

Time	Food	Amount
____	____	____
____	____	____
____	____	____
____	____	____
____	____	____
____	____	____

PM

Time	Food	Amount
____	____	____
____	____	____
____	____	____
____	____	____
____	____	____
____	____	____

SLEEP

AM

Start	End	Duration
____	____	____
____	____	____
____	____	____
____	____	____
____	____	____
____	____	____

PM

Start	End	Duration
____	____	____
____	____	____
____	____	____
____	____	____
____	____	____
____	____	____

DIAPER

Pee	Poop	Time
O	O	____
O	O	____
O	O	____

Pee	Poop	Time
O	O	____
O	O	____
O	O	____

Activity Notes

Baby's Mood

FOOD

AM

Time	Food	Amount

PM

Time	Food	Amount

SLEEP

AM

Start	End	Duration

PM

Start	End	Duration

DIAPER

Pee Poop Time

Pee Poop Time

Activity Notes

Baby's Mood

FOOD

AM

Time	Food	Amount

PM

Time	Food	Amount

SLEEP

AM

Start	End	Duration

PM

Start	End	Duration

DIAPER

Pee	Poop	Time
○	○	
○	○	
○	○	

Pee	Poop	Time
○	○	
○	○	
○	○	

Activity Notes

Baby's Mood

DATE

FOOD

AM

Time	Food	Amount

PM

Time	Food	Amount

SLEEP

AM

Start	End	Duration

PM

Start	End	Duration

DIAPER

Pee	Poop	Time
○	○	
○	○	
○	○	

Pee	Poop	Time
○	○	
○	○	
○	○	

Activity Notes

Baby's Mood

DATE

FOOD

AM

Time	Food	Amount

PM

Time	Food	Amount

SLEEP

AM

Start	End	Duration

PM

Start	End	Duration

DIAPER

Pee	Poop	Time
○	○	
○	○	
○	○	

Pee	Poop	Time
○	○	
○	○	
○	○	

Activity Notes

Baby's Mood

DATE

FOOD

AM

Time	Food	Amount

PM

Time	Food	Amount

SLEEP

AM

Start	End	Duration

PM

Start	End	Duration

DIAPER

Pee	Poop	Time
O	O	
O	O	
O	O	

Pee	Poop	Time
O	O	
O	O	
O	O	

Activity Notes

Baby's Mood

FOOD

AM

Time	Food	Amount

PM

Time	Food	Amount

SLEEP

AM

Start	End	Duration

PM

Start	End	Duration

DIAPER

Pee	Poop	Time
○	○	
○	○	
○	○	

Pee	Poop	Time
○	○	
○	○	
○	○	

Activity Notes

Baby's Mood

DATE

FOOD

AM

Time	Food	Amount

PM

Time	Food	Amount

SLEEP

AM

Start	End	Duration

PM

Start	End	Duration

DIAPER

Pee Poop Time

Pee Poop Time

Activity Notes

Baby's Mood

FOOD

AM

Time	Food	Amount

PM

Time	Food	Amount

SLEEP

AM

Start	End	Duration

PM

Start	End	Duration

DIAPER

Pee	Poop	Time
○	○	
○	○	
○	○	

Pee	Poop	Time
○	○	
○	○	
○	○	

Activity Notes

Baby's Mood

😁 ☹️ 😌 😐 😠

FOOD

AM

Time	Food	Amount

PM

Time	Food	Amount

SLEEP

AM

Start	End	Duration

PM

Start	End	Duration

DIAPER

Pee	Poop	Time
◯	◯	____
◯	◯	____
◯	◯	____

Pee	Poop	Time
◯	◯	____
◯	◯	____
◯	◯	____

Activity Notes

Baby's Mood 😁 ☹ 😌 😐 😠

FOOD

AM

Time	Food	Amount

PM

Time	Food	Amount

SLEEP

AM

Start	End	Duration

PM

Start	End	Duration

DIAPER

Pee	Poop	Time
○	○	__________
○	○	__________
○	○	__________

Pee	Poop	Time
○	○	__________
○	○	__________
○	○	__________

Activity Notes

Baby's Mood

DATE

FOOD

AM

Time	Food	Amount

PM

Time	Food	Amount

SLEEP

AM

Start	End	Duration

PM

Start	End	Duration

DIAPER

Pee Poop Time

○ ○ ____________
○ ○ ____________
○ ○ ____________

Pee Poop Time

○ ○ ____________
○ ○ ____________
○ ○ ____________

Activity Notes

Baby's Mood

DATE

FOOD

AM

Time	Food	Amount

PM

Time	Food	Amount

SLEEP

AM

Start	End	Duration

PM

Start	End	Duration

DIAPER

Pee Poop Time

Pee Poop Time

Activity Notes

Baby's Mood

DATE

FOOD

AM

Time	Food	Amount

PM

Time	Food	Amount

SLEEP

AM

Start	End	Duration

PM

Start	End	Duration

DIAPER

Pee	Poop	Time
◯	◯	
◯	◯	
◯	◯	

Pee	Poop	Time
◯	◯	
◯	◯	
◯	◯	

Activity Notes

Baby's Mood

FOOD

AM

Time	Food	Amount

PM

Time	Food	Amount

SLEEP

AM

Start	End	Duration

PM

Start	End	Duration

DIAPER

Pee	Poop	Time		Pee	Poop	Time
O	O			O	O	
O	O			O	O	
O	O			O	O	

Activity Notes

Baby's Mood

DATE

FOOD

AM

Time	Food	Amount

PM

Time	Food	Amount

SLEEP

AM

Start	End	Duration

PM

Start	End	Duration

DIAPER

Pee	Poop	Time
O	O	
O	O	
O	O	

Pee	Poop	Time
O	O	
O	O	
O	O	

Activity Notes

Baby's Mood 😁 ☹️ 😌 😐 😠

DATE

FOOD

AM

Time	Food	Amount
____	____	____
____	____	____
____	____	____
____	____	____
____	____	____
____	____	____

PM

Time	Food	Amount
____	____	____
____	____	____
____	____	____
____	____	____
____	____	____
____	____	____

SLEEP

AM

Start	End	Duration
____	____	____
____	____	____
____	____	____
____	____	____
____	____	____
____	____	____

PM

Start	End	Duration
____	____	____
____	____	____
____	____	____
____	____	____
____	____	____
____	____	____

DIAPER

Pee Poop Time
○ ○ ________
○ ○ ________
○ ○ ________

Pee Poop Time
○ ○ ________
○ ○ ________
○ ○ ________

Activity Notes

Baby's Mood

DATE

FOOD

AM

Time	Food	Amount

PM

Time	Food	Amount

SLEEP

AM

Start	End	Duration

PM

Start	End	Duration

DIAPER

Pee	Poop	Time
○	○	
○	○	
○	○	

Pee	Poop	Time
○	○	
○	○	
○	○	

Activity Notes

Baby's Mood

DATE

FOOD

AM

Time	Food	Amount

PM

Time	Food	Amount

SLEEP

AM

Start	End	Duration

PM

Start	End	Duration

DIAPER

Pee Poop Time

○ ○ ________

○ ○ ________

○ ○ ________

Pee Poop Time

○ ○ ________

○ ○ ________

○ ○ ________

Activity Notes

Baby's Mood

FOOD

AM

Time	Food	Amount

PM

Time	Food	Amount

SLEEP

AM

Start	End	Duration

PM

Start	End	Duration

DIAPER

Pee	Poop	Time		Pee	Poop	Time
○	○			○	○	
○	○			○	○	
○	○			○	○	

Activity Notes

Baby's Mood

😁 ☹ 😌 😐 😠

FOOD

AM

Time	Food	Amount

PM

Time	Food	Amount

SLEEP

AM

Start	End	Duration

PM

Start	End	Duration

DIAPER

Pee Poop Time

○ ○ ———

○ ○ ———

○ ○ ———

Pee Poop Time

○ ○ ———

○ ○ ———

○ ○ ———

Activity Notes

Baby's Mood 😁 ☹ 😌 😐 😠

FOOD

AM

Time	Food	Amount

PM

Time	Food	Amount

SLEEP

AM

Start	End	Duration

PM

Start	End	Duration

DIAPER

Pee	Poop	Time
○	○	
○	○	
○	○	

Pee	Poop	Time
○	○	
○	○	
○	○	

Activity Notes

Baby's Mood 😁 ☹ 😌 😐 😠

FOOD

AM

Time	Food	Amount
______	______	______
______	______	______
______	______	______
______	______	______
______	______	______
______	______	______

PM

Time	Food	Amount
______	______	______
______	______	______
______	______	______
______	______	______
______	______	______
______	______	______

SLEEP

AM

Start	End	Duration
______	______	______
______	______	______
______	______	______
______	______	______
______	______	______

PM

Start	End	Duration
______	______	______
______	______	______
______	______	______
______	______	______
______	______	______

DIAPER

Pee	Poop	Time
◯	◯	______
◯	◯	______
◯	◯	______

Pee	Poop	Time
◯	◯	______
◯	◯	______
◯	◯	______

Activity Notes

Baby's Mood 😁 ☹️ 😌 😐 😠

FOOD

AM

Time	Food	Amount

PM

Time	Food	Amount

SLEEP

AM

Start	End	Duration

PM

Start	End	Duration

DIAPER

Pee	Poop	Time
○	○	
○	○	
○	○	

Pee	Poop	Time
○	○	
○	○	
○	○	

Activity Notes

Baby's Mood

FOOD

AM

Time	Food	Amount

PM

Time	Food	Amount

SLEEP

AM

Start	End	Duration

PM

Start	End	Duration

DIAPER

Pee Poop — Time

Pee Poop — Time

Activity Notes

Baby's Mood 😁 ☹️ 😌 😐 😠

FOOD

AM

Time	Food	Amount

PM

Time	Food	Amount

SLEEP

AM

Start	End	Duration

PM

Start	End	Duration

DIAPER

Pee Poop   Time

○ ○ ________
○ ○ ________
○ ○ ________

Pee Poop   Time

○ ○ ________
○ ○ ________
○ ○ ________

Activity Notes

Baby's Mood

DATE

FOOD

AM	

Time	Food	Amount

PM	

Time	Food	Amount

SLEEP

AM	

Start	End	Duration

PM	

Start	End	Duration

DIAPER

Pee	Poop	Time

Pee	Poop	Time

Activity Notes

Baby's Mood

FOOD

AM

Time	Food	Amount
_____	_____	_____
_____	_____	_____
_____	_____	_____
_____	_____	_____
_____	_____	_____
_____	_____	_____

PM

Time	Food	Amount
_____	_____	_____
_____	_____	_____
_____	_____	_____
_____	_____	_____
_____	_____	_____
_____	_____	_____

SLEEP

AM

Start	End	Duration
_____	_____	_____
_____	_____	_____
_____	_____	_____
_____	_____	_____
_____	_____	_____
_____	_____	_____

PM

Start	End	Duration
_____	_____	_____
_____	_____	_____
_____	_____	_____
_____	_____	_____
_____	_____	_____
_____	_____	_____

DIAPER

Pee	Poop	Time
◯	◯	_____
◯	◯	_____
◯	◯	_____

Pee	Poop	Time
◯	◯	_____
◯	◯	_____
◯	◯	_____

Activity Notes

Baby's Mood

DATE

FOOD

AM

Time	Food	Amount

PM

Time	Food	Amount

SLEEP

AM

Start	End	Duration

PM

Start	End	Duration

DIAPER

Pee	Poop	Time
○	○	
○	○	
○	○	

Pee	Poop	Time
○	○	
○	○	
○	○	

Activity Notes

Baby's Mood

😁 ☹️ 😌 😐 😠

DATE

FOOD

AM

Time	Food	Amount

PM

Time	Food	Amount

SLEEP

AM

Start	End	Duration

PM

Start	End	Duration

DIAPER

Pee	Poop	Time
○	○	
○	○	
○	○	

Pee	Poop	Time
○	○	
○	○	
○	○	

Activity Notes

Baby's Mood

FOOD

AM

Time	Food	Amount

PM

Time	Food	Amount

SLEEP

AM

Start	End	Duration

PM

Start	End	Duration

DIAPER

Pee	Poop	Time
○	○	———
○	○	———
○	○	———

Pee	Poop	Time
○	○	———
○	○	———
○	○	———

Activity Notes

Baby's Mood 😁 ☹ 😌 😐 😠

FOOD

AM

Time	Food	Amount

PM

Time	Food	Amount

SLEEP

AM

Start	End	Duration

PM

Start	End	Duration

DIAPER

Pee	Poop	Time
○	○	_______
○	○	_______
○	○	_______

Pee	Poop	Time
○	○	_______
○	○	_______
○	○	_______

Activity Notes

Baby's Mood

FOOD

AM

Time	Food	Amount

PM

Time	Food	Amount

SLEEP

AM

Start	End	Duration

PM

Start	End	Duration

DIAPER

Pee	Poop	Time
○	○	
○	○	
○	○	

Pee	Poop	Time
○	○	
○	○	
○	○	

Activity Notes

Baby's Mood 😁 ☹️ 😌 😐 😠

FOOD

AM

Time	Food	Amount

PM

Time	Food	Amount

SLEEP

AM

Start	End	Duration

PM

Start	End	Duration

DIAPER

Pee	Poop	Time
○	○	
○	○	
○	○	

Pee	Poop	Time
○	○	
○	○	
○	○	

Activity Notes

Baby's Mood

😁 ☹ 😌 😐 😠

DATE

FOOD

AM

Time	Food	Amount

PM

Time	Food	Amount

SLEEP

AM

Start	End	Duration

PM

Start	End	Duration

DIAPER

Pee	Poop	Time
◯	◯	______
◯	◯	______
◯	◯	______

Pee	Poop	Time
◯	◯	______
◯	◯	______
◯	◯	______

Activity Notes

Baby's Mood

FOOD

AM

Time	Food	Amount
_____	_____	_____
_____	_____	_____
_____	_____	_____
_____	_____	_____
_____	_____	_____
_____	_____	_____

PM

Time	Food	Amount
_____	_____	_____
_____	_____	_____
_____	_____	_____
_____	_____	_____
_____	_____	_____
_____	_____	_____

SLEEP

AM

Start	End	Duration
_____	_____	_____
_____	_____	_____
_____	_____	_____
_____	_____	_____
_____	_____	_____
_____	_____	_____

PM

Start	End	Duration
_____	_____	_____
_____	_____	_____
_____	_____	_____
_____	_____	_____
_____	_____	_____
_____	_____	_____

DIAPER

Pee	Poop	Time
O	O	_____
O	O	_____
O	O	_____

Pee	Poop	Time
O	O	_____
O	O	_____
O	O	_____

Activity Notes

Baby's Mood

DATE

FOOD

AM

Time	Food	Amount

PM

Time	Food	Amount

SLEEP

AM

Start	End	Duration

PM

Start	End	Duration

DIAPER

Pee Poop Time

Pee Poop Time

Activity Notes

Baby's Mood 😁 ☹ 😌 😐 😠

FOOD

AM

Time	Food	Amount

PM

Time	Food	Amount

SLEEP

AM

Start	End	Duration

PM

Start	End	Duration

DIAPER

Pee	Poop	Time
○	○	
○	○	
○	○	

Pee	Poop	Time
○	○	
○	○	
○	○	

Activity Notes

Baby's Mood

DATE

FOOD

AM

Time	Food	Amount

PM

Time	Food	Amount

SLEEP

AM

Start	End	Duration

PM

Start	End	Duration

DIAPER

Pee	Poop	Time
○	○	
○	○	
○	○	

Pee	Poop	Time
○	○	
○	○	
○	○	

Activity Notes

Baby's Mood

DATE

FOOD

AM

Time	Food	Amount
____	____	____
____	____	____
____	____	____
____	____	____
____	____	____
____	____	____

PM

Time	Food	Amount
____	____	____
____	____	____
____	____	____
____	____	____
____	____	____
____	____	____

SLEEP

AM

Start	End	Duration
____	____	____
____	____	____
____	____	____
____	____	____
____	____	____
____	____	____

PM

Start	End	Duration
____	____	____
____	____	____
____	____	____
____	____	____
____	____	____
____	____	____

DIAPER

Pee	Poop	Time		Pee	Poop	Time
◯	◯	____		◯	◯	____
◯	◯	____		◯	◯	____
◯	◯	____		◯	◯	____

Activity Notes

Baby's Mood

DATE

FOOD

AM

Time	Food	Amount

PM

Time	Food	Amount

SLEEP

AM

Start	End	Duration

PM

Start	End	Duration

DIAPER

Pee	Poop	Time
○	○	
○	○	
○	○	

Pee	Poop	Time
○	○	
○	○	
○	○	

Activity Notes

Baby's Mood 😁 ☹️ 😌 😐 😠

FOOD

AM

Time	Food	Amount

PM

Time	Food	Amount

SLEEP

AM

Start	End	Duration

PM

Start	End	Duration

DIAPER

Pee	Poop	Time
○	○	
○	○	
○	○	

Pee	Poop	Time
○	○	
○	○	
○	○	

Activity Notes

Baby's Mood

DATE

AM   FOOD   PM

Time	Food	Amount		Time	Food	Amount

AM   SLEEP   PM

Start	End	Duration		Start	End	Duration

DIAPER

Pee Poop   Time   Pee Poop   Time

Activity Notes

Baby's Mood 😁 ☹ 😌 😐 😠

DATE

FOOD

AM

Time	Food	Amount

PM

Time	Food	Amount

SLEEP

AM

Start	End	Duration

PM

Start	End	Duration

DIAPER

Pee	Poop	Time
◯	◯	______
◯	◯	______
◯	◯	______

Pee	Poop	Time
◯	◯	______
◯	◯	______
◯	◯	______

Activity Notes

Baby's Mood

DATE

FOOD

AM

Time	Food	Amount

PM

Time	Food	Amount

SLEEP

AM

Start	End	Duration

PM

Start	End	Duration

DIAPER

Pee	Poop	Time
O	O	
O	O	
O	O	

Pee	Poop	Time
O	O	
O	O	
O	O	

Activity Notes

Baby's Mood

FOOD

AM

Time	Food	Amount

PM

Time	Food	Amount

SLEEP

AM

Start	End	Duration

PM

Start	End	Duration

DIAPER

Pee	Poop	Time
O	O	
O	O	
O	O	

Pee	Poop	Time
O	O	
O	O	
O	O	

Activity Notes

Baby's Mood 😁 ☹ 😌 😐 😠

FOOD

AM

Time	Food	Amount

PM

Time	Food	Amount

SLEEP

AM

Start	End	Duration

PM

Start	End	Duration

DIAPER

Pee Poop Time
○ ○ ——————
○ ○ ——————
○ ○ ——————

Pee Poop Time
○ ○ ——————
○ ○ ——————
○ ○ ——————

Activity Notes

Baby's Mood

DATE

FOOD

AM

Time	Food	Amount

PM

Time	Food	Amount

SLEEP

AM

Start	End	Duration

PM

Start	End	Duration

DIAPER

Pee	Poop	Time		Pee	Poop	Time
○	○			○	○	
○	○			○	○	
○	○			○	○	

Activity Notes

Baby's Mood

DATE

FOOD

AM

Time	Food	Amount

PM

Time	Food	Amount

SLEEP

AM

Start	End	Duration

PM

Start	End	Duration

DIAPER

Pee Poop Time

○ ○ ————

○ ○ ————

○ ○ ————

Pee Poop Time

○ ○ ————

○ ○ ————

○ ○ ————

Activity Notes

Baby's Mood

FOOD

AM

Time	Food	Amount

PM

Time	Food	Amount

SLEEP

AM

Start	End	Duration

PM

Start	End	Duration

DIAPER

Pee	Poop	Time
○	○	
○	○	
○	○	

Pee	Poop	Time
○	○	
○	○	
○	○	

Activity Notes

Baby's Mood

😁 🙁 😌 😐 😡

DATE

FOOD

AM

Time	Food	Amount

PM

Time	Food	Amount

SLEEP

AM

Start	End	Duration

PM

Start	End	Duration

DIAPER

Pee Poop Time

Pee Poop Time

Activity Notes

Baby's Mood

DATE

FOOD

AM

Time	Food	Amount

PM

Time	Food	Amount

SLEEP

AM

Start	End	Duration

PM

Start	End	Duration

DIAPER

Pee	Poop	Time		Pee	Poop	Time
○	○			○	○	
○	○			○	○	
○	○			○	○	

Activity Notes

Baby's Mood

FOOD

AM

Time	Food	Amount

PM

Time	Food	Amount

SLEEP

AM

Start	End	Duration

PM

Start	End	Duration

DIAPER

Pee	Poop	Time
○	○	
○	○	
○	○	

Pee	Poop	Time
○	○	
○	○	
○	○	

Activity Notes

Baby's Mood

DATE

FOOD

AM

Time	Food	Amount

PM

Time	Food	Amount

SLEEP

AM

Start	End	Duration

PM

Start	End	Duration

DIAPER

Pee	Poop	Time		Pee	Poop	Time
◯	◯			◯	◯	
◯	◯			◯	◯	
◯	◯			◯	◯	

Activity Notes

Baby's Mood

FOOD

AM

Time	Food	Amount

PM

Time	Food	Amount

SLEEP

AM

Start	End	Duration

PM

Start	End	Duration

DIAPER

Pee Poop   Time

Pee Poop   Time

Activity Notes

Baby's Mood

FOOD

AM

Time	Food	Amount

PM

Time	Food	Amount

SLEEP

AM

Start	End	Duration

PM

Start	End	Duration

DIAPER

Pee Poop Time

Pee Poop Time

Activity Notes

Baby's Mood

DATE

FOOD

AM

Time	Food	Amount

PM

Time	Food	Amount

SLEEP

AM

Start	End	Duration

PM

Start	End	Duration

DIAPER

Pee Poop Time

Pee Poop Time

Activity Notes

Baby's Mood

DATE

FOOD

AM			PM		
Time	Food	Amount	Time	Food	Amount

SLEEP

AM			PM		
Start	End	Duration	Start	End	Duration

DIAPER

Pee Poop	Time	Pee Poop	Time
○ ○	________	○ ○	________
○ ○	________	○ ○	________
○ ○	________	○ ○	________

Activity Notes

Baby's Mood 😁 ☹ 😌 😐 😠

FOOD

AM
Time	Food	Amount

PM
Time	Food	Amount

SLEEP

AM
Start	End	Duration

PM
Start	End	Duration

DIAPER

Pee	Poop	Time
○	○	
○	○	
○	○	

Pee	Poop	Time
○	○	
○	○	
○	○	

Activity Notes

Baby's Mood 😁 ☹ 😌 😐 😠

FOOD

AM

Time	Food	Amount

PM

Time	Food	Amount

SLEEP

AM

Start	End	Duration

PM

Start	End	Duration

DIAPER

Pee	Poop	Time		Pee	Poop	Time
◯	◯			◯	◯	
◯	◯			◯	◯	
◯	◯			◯	◯	

Activity Notes

Baby's Mood 😁 ☹ 😌 😐 😠

DATE

FOOD

AM

Time	Food	Amount

PM

Time	Food	Amount

SLEEP

AM

Start	End	Duration

PM

Start	End	Duration

DIAPER

Pee	Poop	Time
○	○	_____
○	○	_____
○	○	_____

Pee	Poop	Time
○	○	_____
○	○	_____
○	○	_____

Activity Notes

Baby's Mood 😁 ☹ 😌 😐 😠

FOOD

AM

Time	Food	Amount

PM

Time	Food	Amount

SLEEP

AM

Start	End	Duration

PM

Start	End	Duration

DIAPER

Pee	Poop	Time
◯	◯	
◯	◯	
◯	◯	

Pee	Poop	Time
◯	◯	
◯	◯	
◯	◯	

Activity Notes

Baby's Mood

AM   FOOD   PM

| Time | Food | Amount | | Time | Food | Amount |

AM   SLEEP   PM

| Start | End | Duration | | Start | End | Duration |

DIAPER

Pee Poop   Time   Pee Poop   Time

Activity Notes

Baby's Mood

DATE

FOOD

AM
Time	Food	Amount

PM
Time	Food	Amount

SLEEP

AM
Start	End	Duration

PM
Start	End	Duration

DIAPER

Pee Poop Time

Pee Poop Time

Activity Notes

Baby's Mood

DATE

FOOD

AM

Time	Food	Amount

PM

Time	Food	Amount

SLEEP

AM

Start	End	Duration

PM

Start	End	Duration

DIAPER

Pee Poop Time

Pee Poop Time

Activity Notes

Baby's Mood

DATE

FOOD

AM

Time	Food	Amount

PM

Time	Food	Amount

SLEEP

AM

Start	End	Duration

PM

Start	End	Duration

DIAPER

Pee	Poop	Time
○	○	
○	○	
○	○	

Pee	Poop	Time
○	○	
○	○	
○	○	

Activity Notes

Baby's Mood 😁 ☹ 😌 😐 😠

FOOD

AM

Time	Food	Amount

PM

Time	Food	Amount

SLEEP

AM

Start	End	Duration

PM

Start	End	Duration

DIAPER

Pee	Poop	Time
○	○	
○	○	
○	○	

Pee	Poop	Time
○	○	
○	○	
○	○	

Activity Notes

Baby's Mood 😁 ☹ 😌 😐 😠

FOOD

AM				PM		
Time	Food	Amount		Time	Food	Amount

SLEEP

AM				PM		
Start	End	Duration		Start	End	Duration

DIAPER

Pee	Poop	Time		Pee	Poop	Time

Activity Notes

Baby's Mood

DATE

FOOD

AM

Time	Food	Amount

PM

Time	Food	Amount

SLEEP

AM

Start	End	Duration

PM

Start	End	Duration

DIAPER

Pee Poop Time

Pee Poop Time

Activity Notes

Baby's Mood

😁 ☹ 😌 😐 😠

DATE

FOOD

AM

Time	Food	Amount

PM

Time	Food	Amount

SLEEP

AM

Start	End	Duration

PM

Start	End	Duration

DIAPER

Pee	Poop	Time		Pee	Poop	Time
○	○			○	○	
○	○			○	○	
○	○			○	○	

Activity Notes

Baby's Mood 😁 ☹ 😌 😐 😠

FOOD

AM

Time	Food	Amount

PM

Time	Food	Amount

SLEEP

AM

Start	End	Duration

PM

Start	End	Duration

DIAPER

Pee	Poop	Time
○	○	
○	○	
○	○	

Pee	Poop	Time
○	○	
○	○	
○	○	

Activity Notes

Baby's Mood 😁 ☹ 😌 😐 😠   DATE

FOOD

AM

Time	Food	Amount

PM

Time	Food	Amount

SLEEP

AM

Start	End	Duration

PM

Start	End	Duration

DIAPER

Pee	Poop	Time		Pee	Poop	Time
○	○	_____		○	○	_____
○	○	_____		○	○	_____
○	○	_____		○	○	_____

Activity Notes

Baby's Mood

FOOD

AM

Time	Food	Amount

PM

Time	Food	Amount

SLEEP

AM

Start	End	Duration

PM

Start	End	Duration

DIAPER

Pee	Poop	Time
○	○	
○	○	
○	○	

Pee	Poop	Time
○	○	
○	○	
○	○	

Activity Notes

Baby's Mood   😁 ☹️ 😌 😐 😠

FOOD

AM

Time	Food	Amount

PM

Time	Food	Amount

SLEEP

AM

Start	End	Duration

PM

Start	End	Duration

DIAPER

Pee Poop   Time

Pee Poop   Time

Activity Notes

Baby's Mood 😁 ☹ 😌 😐 😠

FOOD

AM

Time	Food	Amount

PM

Time	Food	Amount

SLEEP

AM

Start	End	Duration

PM

Start	End	Duration

DIAPER

Pee	Poop	Time
○	○	
○	○	
○	○	

Pee	Poop	Time
○	○	
○	○	
○	○	

Activity Notes

Baby's Mood

DATE

FOOD

AM

Time	Food	Amount

PM

Time	Food	Amount

SLEEP

AM

Start	End	Duration

PM

Start	End	Duration

DIAPER

Pee	Poop	Time
O	O	
O	O	
O	O	

Pee	Poop	Time
O	O	
O	O	
O	O	

Activity Notes

Baby's Mood

😁 ☹ 😌 😐 😠

FOOD

AM

Time	Food	Amount

PM

Time	Food	Amount

SLEEP

AM

Start	End	Duration

PM

Start	End	Duration

DIAPER

Pee Poop Time

Pee Poop Time

Activity Notes

Baby's Mood 😁 ☹ 😌 😐 😠

DATE

FOOD

AM

Time	Food	Amount

PM

Time	Food	Amount

SLEEP

AM

Start	End	Duration

PM

Start	End	Duration

DIAPER

Pee	Poop	Time
○	○	
○	○	
○	○	

Pee	Poop	Time
○	○	
○	○	
○	○	

Activity Notes

Baby's Mood

😁 ☹ 😌 😐 😠

FOOD

AM
Time	Food	Amount

PM
Time	Food	Amount

SLEEP

AM
Start	End	Duration

PM
Start	End	Duration

DIAPER

Pee	Poop	Time
○	○	
○	○	
○	○	

Pee	Poop	Time
○	○	
○	○	
○	○	

Activity Notes

Baby's Mood

😁 ☹️ 😌 😐 😠

DATE

FOOD

AM

Time	Food	Amount

PM

Time	Food	Amount

SLEEP

AM

Start	End	Duration

PM

Start	End	Duration

DIAPER

Pee Poop   Time

○ ○ ___________
○ ○ ___________
○ ○ ___________

Pee Poop   Time

○ ○ ___________
○ ○ ___________
○ ○ ___________

Activity Notes

Baby's Mood

DATE

FOOD

AM

Time	Food	Amount

PM

Time	Food	Amount

SLEEP

AM

Start	End	Duration

PM

Start	End	Duration

DIAPER

Pee	Poop	Time
O	O	
O	O	
O	O	

Pee	Poop	Time
O	O	
O	O	
O	O	

Activity Notes

Baby's Mood

DATE

FOOD

AM

Time	Food	Amount

PM

Time	Food	Amount

SLEEP

AM

Start	End	Duration

PM

Start	End	Duration

DIAPER

Pee	Poop	Time
O	O	
O	O	
O	O	

Pee	Poop	Time
O	O	
O	O	
O	O	

Activity Notes

Baby's Mood

DATE

FOOD

AM

Time	Food	Amount

PM

Time	Food	Amount

SLEEP

AM

Start	End	Duration

PM

Start	End	Duration

DIAPER

Pee	Poop	Time
○	○	
○	○	
○	○	

Pee	Poop	Time
○	○	
○	○	
○	○	

Activity Notes

Baby's Mood

😁 ☹ 😌 😐 😠

FOOD

AM

Time	Food	Amount

PM

Time	Food	Amount

SLEEP

AM

Start	End	Duration

PM

Start	End	Duration

DIAPER

Pee	Poop	Time		Pee	Poop	Time
◯	◯			◯	◯	
◯	◯			◯	◯	
◯	◯			◯	◯	

Activity Notes

Baby's Mood

DATE

FOOD

AM

Time	Food	Amount

PM

Time	Food	Amount

SLEEP

AM

Start	End	Duration

PM

Start	End	Duration

DIAPER

Pee Poop Time
O O _______
O O _______
O O _______

Pee Poop Time
O O _______
O O _______
O O _______

Activity Notes

Baby's Mood

😁 ☹ 😌 😐 😠

DATE

FOOD

AM

Time	Food	Amount
___	___	___
___	___	___
___	___	___
___	___	___
___	___	___
___	___	___

PM

Time	Food	Amount
___	___	___
___	___	___
___	___	___
___	___	___
___	___	___
___	___	___

SLEEP

AM

Start	End	Duration
___	___	___
___	___	___
___	___	___
___	___	___
___	___	___
___	___	___

PM

Start	End	Duration
___	___	___
___	___	___
___	___	___
___	___	___
___	___	___
___	___	___

DIAPER

Pee	Poop	Time
◯	◯	___
◯	◯	___
◯	◯	___

Pee	Poop	Time
◯	◯	___
◯	◯	___
◯	◯	___

Activity Notes

Baby's Mood

DATE

FOOD

AM

Time	Food	Amount

PM

Time	Food	Amount

SLEEP

AM

Start	End	Duration

PM

Start	End	Duration

DIAPER

Pee Poop Time

O O ———————
O O ———————
O O ———————

Pee Poop Time

O O ———————
O O ———————
O O ———————

Activity Notes

Baby's Mood

FOOD

AM

Time	Food	Amount

PM

Time	Food	Amount

SLEEP

AM

Start	End	Duration

PM

Start	End	Duration

DIAPER

Pee	Poop	Time
O	O	
O	O	
O	O	

Pee	Poop	Time
O	O	
O	O	
O	O	

Activity Notes

Baby's Mood

DATE

FOOD

AM

Time	Food	Amount

PM

Time	Food	Amount

SLEEP

AM

Start	End	Duration

PM

Start	End	Duration

DIAPER

Pee Poop   Time

○ ○ __________
○ ○ __________
○ ○ __________

Pee Poop   Time

○ ○ __________
○ ○ __________
○ ○ __________

Activity Notes

Baby's Mood

FOOD

AM

Time	Food	Amount

PM

Time	Food	Amount

SLEEP

AM

Start	End	Duration

PM

Start	End	Duration

DIAPER

Pee Poop   Time

Pee Poop   Time

Activity Notes

Baby's Mood

😁 ☹ 😌 😐 😠

DATE

FOOD

AM

Time	Food	Amount

PM

Time	Food	Amount

SLEEP

AM

Start	End	Duration

PM

Start	End	Duration

DIAPER

Pee	Poop	Time
○	○	
○	○	
○	○	

Pee	Poop	Time
○	○	
○	○	
○	○	

Activity Notes

Baby's Mood

FOOD

AM

Time	Food	Amount

PM

Time	Food	Amount

SLEEP

AM

Start	End	Duration

PM

Start	End	Duration

DIAPER

Pee Poop   Time

Pee Poop   Time

Activity Notes

Baby's Mood

DATE

FOOD

AM

Time	Food	Amount

PM

Time	Food	Amount

SLEEP

AM

Start	End	Duration

PM

Start	End	Duration

DIAPER

Pee	Poop	Time
◯	◯	
◯	◯	
◯	◯	

Pee	Poop	Time
◯	◯	
◯	◯	
◯	◯	

Activity Notes

Baby's Mood

DATE

FOOD

AM

Time	Food	Amount

PM

Time	Food	Amount

SLEEP

AM

Start	End	Duration

PM

Start	End	Duration

DIAPER

Pee	Poop	Time		Pee	Poop	Time
◯	◯			◯	◯	
◯	◯			◯	◯	
◯	◯			◯	◯	

Activity Notes

Baby's Mood

DATE

FOOD

AM

Time	Food	Amount

PM

Time	Food	Amount

SLEEP

AM

Start	End	Duration

PM

Start	End	Duration

DIAPER

Pee Poop Time

Pee Poop Time

Activity Notes

Baby's Mood

DATE

FOOD

AM

Time	Food	Amount

PM

Time	Food	Amount

SLEEP

AM

Start	End	Duration

PM

Start	End	Duration

DIAPER

Pee	Poop	Time
O	O	
O	O	
O	O	

Pee	Poop	Time
O	O	
O	O	
O	O	

Activity Notes